Taking "No"
for an Answer and Other Skills Children Need
Fifty Games to Teach Family Skills

Laurie Simons, M.A.
Illustrated by Dave Garbot
Foreword by Phyllis B. Booth

Parenting Press, Inc.
Seattle, Washington

Library of Congress Cataloging-in-Publication Data
Simons, Laurie, 1951-
     Taking "no" for an answer and other skills children need : fifty games to teach family skills / Laurie Simons ; illustrated by Dave Garbot.
        p.   cm.
     Includes index.
     ISBN 1-884734-45-6. -- ISBN 1-884734-44-8 (pbk.)
     1. Child rearing. 2. Parenting. 3. Educational games.
I. Title.
HQ769.S5493 2000
649'.1--dc21   99-41521

Author's note: I thank the Theraplay Institute (www.theraplay.org) for the ideas in games 3 and 16.

Parenting Press, Inc.
P.O. Box 75267
Seattle, Washington 98175
www.ParentingPress.com

PTGAR

Contents

An Invitation

The instructions for playing the games often refer to "parent" or "parents." All the games can be played by *any interested adult* who cares for or about a child. This book is for grandparents, aunts, uncles, teachers, counselors, nannies, day care providers, family friends, etc. as well as parents of all kinds.

Foreword

The most powerful way that families can build unity, cooperation, and respect for others is through play. This book with its rich variety of playful games is designed to promote healthy interaction. It is in playful interaction that we learn about ourselves and become aware of others–play that includes taking turns, following rules, keeping agreements, cooperating with others, and above all, having fun.

Based on the developmental tasks that all children need to master, Laurie Simons has developed fifty games to help children practice the skills they need to become healthy, happy, productive adults. The emphasis in this upbeat, positive book is on learning skills and preventing problems, not on treatment.

These games do not simply promote superficial politeness; they convey a genuinely caring and respectful attitude toward others. Starting with activities that help the child feel safe, valued, and understood, the games progress through a series that help children learn that others matter, too. Taking "no" for an answer, for example, is a skill that everyone who respects the rights of others must have. These playful games help children learn skills without feeling shame or loss of self-esteem.

In this day of super-busy families, where work and getting ahead seem to have edged out the values of caring and respecting others, and of playing together, this book presents a delightful approach to learning skills every child needs. Families in which all members play together as they learn stand an excellent chance of avoiding the alienation and anger that plague our achievement-driven society.

Although designed for families to enjoy without professional help, this book will make a wonderful addition to the repertoire of family therapists, teachers, and others working with groups of children.

Phyllis B. Booth, M.A.
The Theraplay Institute

Dear Reader

Hello! Thanks for picking up this little book. I hope it gives you hours of delight with your family and makes parenting a joy for you. Let me tell you why I wrote it.

I always wanted to be a parent. As a child, I played with dolls to practice the art. Then, at age 22, I became a foster parent to a 7-year-old boy named Perry, who had many behavior problems. I was hurt and resentful when he rejected me. I felt like a failure. I couldn't sleep at night. I needed help!

After eight months, Perry went back to live with his family. I started taking parenting classes, and eventually began teaching them. By the time I had my first child, I was a professional psychologist and figured that meant my child should be perfect. He should sleep through the night and never have tantrums and never fight with his brother and always listen to his parents and always do his chores cheerfully and keep his room clean and so on. Well, as you might guess, life was not that easy. Jay and his brother Jeff are now teenagers, and I have to give them credit for teaching me how to be a parent to real kids.

I spent years learning about skills and strategies that parents can use to cope with problems *after they occur.* Then I began to wonder if some of these problems could be avoided. I looked at dozens of families to see what the effective parents were doing and discovered that they were teaching skills to their children. You can do this too, in an enjoyable way, by using the games in this book.

These games help families learn and practice important skills that children will use in all their relationships throughout their lives. If you believe your family is already doing well at these skills, then the games in this book will help you continue to enhance your relationships and cope with developmental changes as your children grow. If you think your family could improve its relationships, playing these games can help problems fall away naturally as you change old habits.

The families I work with have fun playing these games together. I hope you will, too!

Getting Started

These games are for families with children of all ages, but are best suited to children between three and twelve years of age. They are most effective and enjoyable if the whole family plays together. As few as two people can play most of them.

Some games may seem too old or too young for your child. In fact, most of the games can be adapted to suit any age. Remember that older children like to be "babied" once in a while. Younger children will catch on to more complicated games if they have the chance to watch and learn as they go.

The earlier games in the book are aimed at younger children and later ones are well suited to older children. As your child grows, he or she will develop the twelve skills more or less in the order they appear in this book. You can play the games in any order you wish; however, you may discover that some skills you passed over need more practice. The last skill, resolving conflicts, requires the use of the previous eleven skills to be effective.

Here are the twelve skills you can practice through playing these games:

1. Feeling safe and relaxed, trusting
2. Respecting boundaries
3. Making requests
4. Listening
5. Taking "no" for an answer
6. Following directions
7. Acknowledging others
8. Planning
9. Making and keeping agreements
10. Cooperating
11. Solving problems
12. Resolving conflicts

Parents' Guide to Social Skills Development

This table will help you understand how and when your child is best able to learn the skills presented in the games.

Age	Skill	Development
Baby	Trust	Learns that others routinely meet her needs for food, warmth, comfort, interaction.
Toddler	Respect boundaries	Learns that he is separate from Mommy. Learns that his body and possessions are his own and are to be respected, and others have their own bodies and possessions that need to be respected, too. Cannot learn the concept of "sharing" until he has learned the concept of "mine."
Toddler	Make requests	Starts to use words to get what she wants or needs.
Toddler-Teen	Listen to others	Becomes more sociable. Learns to pay attention to the wants, needs, and feelings of other people, which he discovers may be different from his own.
Toddler-Teen	Take "no" for an answer	Learns to cope with disappointment. Learns that she is not being rejected because someone says "no" or thinks differently from her.
Toddler-Teen	Follow directions	Learns to follow directions exactly when that is required. Learns the difference between a request (when he may answer "yes" or "no") and a direction (when he follows it without argument).
School age	Acknowledge others	Learns to appreciate others and to thank them.
Preschool-Teen	Plan	Learns to plan daily activities or special events and to work with others to make a plan.
School age-Teen	Keep agreements	Becomes more responsible, as shown by the ability to make and keep agreements, such as coming home on time or doing a task.

Age	Skill	Development
School age-Teen	Cooperate	Learns to cooperate in order to work with others toward a common goal or task, instead of competing as a loner.
School age-Teen	Solve problems	Learns to work with others to overcome obstacles and solve problems together.
School age-Teen	Resolve conflicts	Learns appropriate ways to channel anger and resolve problems without aggression or bullying.

Three Ways Families Behave

You will be more successful and have more fun with these games when you understand how your family may be behaving.

Who is in charge?

Every family has at least two generations and sometimes more. Each generation has its job to do: children grow up and develop into mature adults, parents guide their children in this process, grandparents enjoy their grandchildren, offer back-up care when needed, and pass on their wisdom.

If the boundaries between generations are clear, parents are in charge of what happens in their family, not the children. When I watch families play these games, I look to see who is in charge. Here is an example of one family playing some of the games in my office:

The parents of 8-year-old Ashley and 12-year-old Tyler sought help because their daughter Ashley always wanted things her way, didn't listen to her parents, and constantly bothered her brother. Tyler wouldn't play with his friends at his house, in fact, he didn't want to be at home at all. Ashley refused to do anything with her dad and always insisted that her mom put her to bed. Everyone felt angry and resentful and said Ashley was no fun to be around.

I asked the family to play this game in which Dad is giving directions to the others. This is how it went:

"Ashley, do you want to go and sit in that chair?"

Ashley ignored Dad and continued to play with the Hula Hoop®.

"Ashley, I'm supposed to be giving you directions, and so could you please go and sit in that chair?"

Ashley said, "Just watch, I'll show you a trick with the Hula Hoop®."

Dad watched patiently and then tried again. "Okay, honey, now would you please go to sit in that chair?"

Ashley said, "Just a minute. I think I'd like to try this other chair first."

Five minutes passed before Ashley went to sit in the chair her father indicated. Meanwhile, Mom and Tyler waited patiently.

After several sessions of playing games that emphasized following directions and having parents in charge, this family played the same game again. Here is how it went this time, with Dad again in charge of giving directions:

"Okay, Ashley, I want you to sit over here in this chair."

Dad took Ashley by the hand and led her to the chair. On the way, she tried to sit in a different chair.

"We are going to this chair," said Dad, accomplishing his goal in 15 seconds. He also placed Mom and Tyler in chairs. Ashley remained in her chair.

"Now I need to pick someone else to be in charge," said Dad. Ashley remained in her chair instead of jumping up to demand she be chosen as she would have done in the past. She raised her hand, as did Tyler. Dad decided Tyler would be next to give directions.

"Darn," said Ashley, remaining in her chair and waiting for Tyler's directions.

Ashley's parents learned to be in charge. Ashley learned about respecting boundaries and how to ask permission if she wanted to play with Tyler and his friends. She learned to respect Tyler's wishes if he said "No." These changes did not happen overnight, but came quickly enough to be rewarding.

Are there "triangles" in your family?

When a third person gets involved between two people who ought to be talking to each other, you have a triangle. Also, when a third person takes sides or tries to solve the problem between two other people, you have a triangle. Here is an example of a family with a triangle problem:

The parents of 9-year-old Katie, 7-year-old Sean, and 5-year-old Kevin sought help because they were exhausted from trying to keep peace among their three children.

In the first visit in which the family played games, I noticed that the parents were clearly in charge and the children behaved very well while the parents were involved in the games. So I looked for other skills the family might need. Here is what happened when Mom and Dad were not part of the game:

Mom and Dad sat at the side of the room reading newspapers. Katie, Sean, and Kevin had five minutes to invent a family game together using the items provided. They had five beanbags, five baskets, an 8-foot length of rope, and a scarf. The timer was set for five minutes.

"I want to jump rope," Sean said.

"No, Sean, we're not going to jump rope," said Katie, as she grabbed the rope away.

"Hey, let me have that," demanded Kevin, who also grabbed the rope and began to pull.

They pulled and tugged and yanked for the full five minutes.

The timer rang.

"We aren't finished," said Kevin.

"We need more time," said Katie.

Sean just kept trying to pull the rope away from Katie.

As you can see, these children needed skills in getting along. Mom and Dad were embarrassed and admitted that one of them usually intervened when the children fought. After six sessions with this family practicing several skills, this is how the children played:

Mom and Dad were reading magazines while the three children looked over the toys.

"May I play with the blue beanbag?" asked Katie, waiting for her brothers to respond.

"Yes," said Sean. "Yes," said Kevin.

Katie reached inside the circle and took the beanbag.

Then Kevin said," May I play with the rope?" He looked to Sean for an answer.

"Yes," said Sean.

"Katie?" asked Kevin.

"Yes," Katie answered.

Kevin then got the rope and began to play with it. Sean looked at all the toys remaining in the circle. He said, "Katie, may I play with the ball?"

Both Katie and Kevin said, "Yes."

Then Katie asked her brothers if she could play with the scarf. The game continued with the children practicing asking permission of one another.

Before the children arrived at this point, they did not always say "Yes" to each other. In fact, in one session Sean said "No" to both his siblings for 20 minutes! Katie and Kevin were encouraged to keep asking politely for the item they wanted. Eventually Sean realized holding out was not necessary nor fun. Once he started saying "Yes" he discovered his siblings were more fun to be with. All three children learned that if someone said "No," it was respected by the sibling. They learned how to cooperate and solve problems on their own. The parents learned how to stay out of the middle, though they did coach the children in the skills they needed to get along together.

Are you a proactive or a reactive parent?

In some families, parents teach children the skills they need in a planned manner before trouble arises. When a problem occurs, parents and children have words to use and the ability to stop and think about how they want to solve the problem. These parents ask questions such as, "How can I teach my children to ask politely, follow directions, or get along together?" These are proactive parents.

In other families, parents react to a problem when it occurs. Children learn that they can get attention by creating problems. Parents who react ask questions such as, "What should I do when my children whine, argue, fight, or don't listen?"

Here is an example of a family who changed its approach from reactive to proactive:

The parents of 12-year-old Steven, 9-year-old Brandon, and 3-year-old Matthew sought help because Matthew was always getting into his brothers' things. Every time he took something of Steven's or Brandon's, he had to sit in his time-out chair. His parents noticed that Matthew's behavior did not change, no matter how many times he had to sit in the chair.

After practicing games to respect boundaries, make requests, and take "no" for an answer, Matthew, young as he was, was able to use these skills when he wanted something from his brothers. Now Steven and Brandon like their brother much better because he respects their possessions.

Tips for Playing the Games

Families who play the games in this book all get to practice the skills together. Your children will start to learn new words and phrases like "Please respect my boundaries," or "Do you have a request?" Once children can use the skills in the games, they will transfer the skills to daily life. For example, the skill of respecting boundaries (no eavesdropping or snooping in rooms or drawers or cabinets) and the skill of making requests ("May I have/do . . . ?") come in handy when your child visits the neighbors or her grandparents.

Not all children like all the games. That is okay; play the ones that are most interesting now and try the others again later. You can change items to play with, too. If a problem comes up while you are playing a game, think carefully about what led up to it. The child who leaves the room in a huff or fights over a toy may need practice with skills that precede the one you are working on at the moment. Play the games that will help him practice the skill he needs.

And remember, have fun!

Feeling Safe and Relaxed, Trusting

Our family is the home base from which we grow and develop into mature and responsible adults. As we grow up and venture out into the world, we rely on returning to the safe haven of our home and family. Children who do not feel safe from hurt or criticism in their own homes can develop problems with anger, anxiety, loneliness, or marriage failure later in life.

Trusting is a skill children learn by having early experiences of being cared for and seen as special. When you trust the people in your family, you feel relaxed, safe, and secure. It is never too late to have these experiences. Even adults benefit from the good feelings these experiences bring.

Some children do not like to relax and let others take care of them. They try to control what happens instead of letting adults be in charge. They may even reject parents' attempts to comfort or nurture them. These children need to practice how to relax, slow down, and enjoy being cared for by their parents.

Play these games if you want family members to:

◆ Feel special
◆ Feel okay when a new baby arrives
◆ Use kind words instead of put-downs
◆ Accept more comfort and nurturing from one another
◆ Enjoy each other instead of feeling resentful or angry
◆ Be considerate of one another

- Take care of one another, instead of hurting one another by hitting, kicking, biting, pinching, throwing things, or other aggressive acts
- Stick together instead of going off to be alone
- Calm down when they get too excited or agitated

Tips for Feeling Safe and Relaxed

- Look for positive aspects in one another. If a child fights being nurtured, for example, comment on how strong her muscles are.
- Pay close attention to body language for clues about how someone feels. Teach children to read each other's body language: facial expressions, stiffness, arms folded across chest or placed behind back, body turned away. These clues will tell them when the other person feels unsafe.
- Keep interactions calm and nurturing. If a child is too excited to participate in an activity or game, look for ways to help him calm down before you continue.

- Speak kindly; avoid teasing and sarcasm. Even when done in a spirit of fun, teasing makes people feel unsure. They may feel the need to withdraw or to protect themselves. Some parents play a teasing game of snatching away the spoon when the baby is about to take a bite. This is not fun for the baby.
- Use encouragement instead of criticism. Sometimes we feel the best way to help another person is to point out their faults. This rarely helps people because they can only change when they feel good about themselves and have self-confidence. Instead of criticizing, try saying encouraging things and ignoring the faults.
- Emphasize the importance of home being a safe place for everyone in the family. Be attentive to words or actions that might make other family members feel unsafe. Do what is necessary to eliminate them.

1 *Swing High, Swing Low*

Trusting

Play game 1 to establish trust among all family members, and to encourage brothers and sisters to nurture each other.

Set-up

Space to play
Sturdy blanket

Directions

1. Two parents hold the corners at each end of the blanket. Children who are tall enough and strong enough may take a turn at holding the blanket corners. Children may also help by holding the sides of the blanket.

2. One child sits or lies in the center of the blanket.

3. Swing your child gently with a smooth and soothing rhythm. Hum or sing a familiar, relaxing song or rhyme.

4. Tell the other children to watch the face of the child in the blanket. Ask them, "Do you think [name] likes this game?" Have them ask, "Do you like this game? Would you like us to swing slower [or faster]?" and so on.

5. Set your child down gently when the turn is over.

6. Give each child in the family a turn swinging in the blanket.

2 Yum, Yum

Trusting

Play game 2 to encourage nurturing, relaxing, and feeling special as the center of attention.

Set-up

Comfortable place for adults to sit
Favorite finger food at least the size of a postage stamp, such as chips, pretzels, pieces of fruit or vegetables, etc.

Directions

1. Put your child on your lap and make her as comfortable as possible.

2. The other parent feeds her the finger food, one piece at a time. (Or one parent can both hold and feed her.)

3. Your child does not touch the food, but simply takes it into her mouth.

4. The parent feeding the child interprets her body language and words to see if she is ready for more, if the piece of food is just right, if she likes it, etc.

5. The game is finished when the food is all gone or your child shows or says she does not want any more.

Note: If your children are too old to play the game this way, play it by having everyone take turns being fed, including the parents.

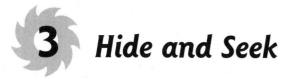

3 Hide and Seek

Trusting

Play game 3 to assure children that they are very special.

Set-up

Two rooms
Large pillows
Blanket

Directions

1. One parent and one child hide under the pillows and the blanket in one room. (Or the child can hide alone while the parent waits in the other room.)

2. The other parent, and siblings, wait in the second room until called.

3. The hiding parent and child yell out, "Come and find us!"

4. The searchers look all over the room, pretending to be baffled. They say things like, "Where is that kid with the wide smile and the long eyelashes?" or "Where is that girl/boy who likes ice cream?" Finally, they find the child and parent and say with great excitement, "Here you are!"

5. Repeat the game until each child in the family has hidden under the blankets and pillows and been found. You can use other hiding places if your child is old enough.

4 Rag Doll

Relaxing
Play game 4 to help children learn strategies for calming themselves when they feel excited or anxious.

Set-up
Space to play

Directions
1. Everyone sits in a circle.

2. One parent gives these instructions:

   a. "Let's do the calming countdown exercise."

   b. "Raise both arms straight up over your head."

   c. "Count with me slowly backwards from ten to one. Lower your arms slowly forward as we count, until they are relaxed and resting on your knees as you say 'one.'"

3. Start counting, choosing the pace for the children to follow.

4. Parents and children lower arms slowly to knees.

5. Say, "I'll check to see if your arms are relaxed," as you lift each child's arm gently by the wrist and let it drop again. Repeat this game until everyone's arms are loose and relaxed.

Respecting Boundaries

One of the basic skills necessary for family success is the ability of family members to be aware of and to respect one another's boundaries. Each family member has his or her own space, identity, opinions, and feelings. In healthy families this space is respected, and these individual differences are celebrated.

Respecting boundaries means that you do not physically invade another person's space, take items belonging to that person without permission, or say insulting things (verbal put-downs). As children grow and develop, they need to know that their boundaries and wishes are respected, and that it is okay to say "no" to someone who infringes on their space, their body, or their possessions.

Note: Before a toddler can know what it means to share, she first needs to know that her own space will be protected from invasion by others. Between ages one and three she is learning what her body boundaries are and what is "mine." Being possessive at this age is normal. Once she knows that her time with a toy, for example, will be respected and uninterrupted, she will be more willing to give someone else a chance to play with it. She is unlikely to understand the concept of "sharing" until she is four or five years old.

Play these games if you want family members to:

- Wait for permission before touching or taking something someone else owns or is using
- Respect the personal (body) space of others

- Leave the belongings of other people alone
- Touch each other in welcome ways
- Learn ways to get along without fighting over toys or other things
- Discover and protect their own boundaries

Tips for Respecting Boundaries

- Use these games to teach vocabulary words such as "personal space," "invading my boundary," etc. This vocabulary will be helpful as children grow up and need to set boundaries or describe inappropriate boundary violations that occur with family members, friends, acquaintances, or strangers.
- Respect everyone's right to say "no" when protecting personal space or property. Space can be the chair they are sitting on, the plate their food is on, their bedroom, their time in the bathroom, etc. Property can be the toy they are playing with at that moment, the magazine they are reading, the cookie they are eating, their clothes, items given specifically to them, etc.
- Speak kindly; avoid put-downs or disrespectful comments. These are a type of boundary violation. Comments like "You're a fatso," "You can't do anything right," "You're a crybaby," "Do I always have to _____ for you?" are harmful.
- Respect the boundary of someone who does not want to play one of these games. Do not attempt to force, cajole, browbeat, or embarrass anyone into playing. Instead, move on to another player. (If this pattern of non-participation is a common theme for the family member, you may need professional advice.)
- Use props that are age appropriate and interesting to the children. If there is a wide age span among the children, make sure the items used are safe for the youngest among them.

5 I'm Stuck on You

Respecting Boundaries
Play game 5 to let children know that their bodies are their own.

Set-up
Space to play
Two stickers for each player from a package of colored dots or other stickers

Directions
1. Sit on the floor in a circle.

2. Start the game by asking a child, "I would like to put this sticker on you. Where would you like me to put it?"

3. If the child says "No," he does not want a sticker put on him, respect his answer and choose someone else to ask. Keep asking until someone agrees.

4. Place the sticker where that person tells you*.

5. Then the turn goes to the person who wears a sticker. Give him a sticker to place on someone else.

6. Continue the game until every family member has had two chances to both receive and to place a sticker on someone.

* Respect your child's wishes regarding where he wants the sticker, unless the spot is inappropriate or "private." In that case, say,

"That's a private spot. Pick another spot, please." If he insists, go on to another player for the time being. Later, after the game is over, have a talk about private parts of the body.

Note: Children have the right to decide whether or not, and where, they want to be touched by other people. The only exception to this is if you need to give first aid or a medical person needs to touch to discover illness or injury, in which case a parent should be present (not always possible in some kinds of emergencies).

6 *See the Boundary*

Respecting Boundaries

Play game 6 to show children what a boundary looks like, because it is easier for them to understand it when they can see and touch it.

Set-up

Space to play

Masking tape

Collection of small toys in a container (two toys for each player). These toys are reserved for this game and should not belong to any of the children.

Directions

1. Stick a circle of masking tape (about four feet in diameter) on the floor in the middle of the room.

2. Everyone sits on the floor outside the circle of tape.

3. Pick one player to sit on the floor inside the masking tape circle. Other players remain outside the boundary. A young child may need to practice sitting or standing at the edge of the tape, with toes just outside the line, to experience the boundary.

4. The player inside the circle holds the basket of toys. She shows the toys one at a time to the other family members, so they will know what toys are available.

5. A parent chooses one of the players on the outside of the circle to go first. This child makes a polite request for one of the toys, saying, "May I have the [item], please?"

6. The person inside the circle decides whether to say "Yes" or "No." If "yes," then she reaches outside the circle to hand over the toy that was requested.

7. The next player to the left asks for a toy.

8. Continue until all the players have had two turns to ask, or until all the toys are gone.

9. Then the person inside the circle collects the toys from all the players and leaves them in the basket, inside the circle. This person leaves the circle and chooses someone else to sit inside the circle with the toys.

10. Continue until each player has had a turn inside the circle boundary.

Note: It is okay for a child to be upset that she did not get a toy. You can sympathize and offer comfort, "You really wanted that toy." Do not give in, however, because you will teach that unpleasant behavior gets her what she wants. She will have another chance as you continue the game.

7 Red Light, Green Light

Respecting Boundaries

Play game 7 to help your child feel and see a real boundary around himself or herself.

Set-up

Space to play
Masking tape and Hula Hoop®

Directions

1. Place a line of masking tape along one end of the room or space.

2. One family member stands at the other end of the room or space, inside the Hula Hoop, holding it horizontally at waist level with both hands.

3. Everyone else stands behind the line of masking tape.

4. When the person in the Hula Hoop® says "Green light!" all the other players begin moving closer. When she says "Red light!" all players must stand still.

5. Anyone who does not stop must return to the starting line and begin again.

6. When players get to the hoop, they must stand outside it and hold on to it with both hands until everyone else has arrived.

7. Continue playing until all family members have had a turn standing inside the Hula Hoop®.

8 Captain, May I?

Respecting Boundaries

Play game 8 to help children learn to notice and respect personal (body) boundaries.

Set-up

Space to play
Masking tape or a Hula Hoop®

Directions

1. Stick a circle of masking tape (about four feet in diameter) on the floor in the middle of the room, or lay the Hula Hoop® in the middle of the floor space.

2. Pick one family member to stand inside the tape boundary or the Hula Hoop® circle.

3. The first player stands with his toes outside the circle and says, "May I touch your shoulder?"

4. He waits for a response from the person in the circle. If the answer is "Yes," he reaches into the circle and gently touches the person's shoulder. If the answer is "No," then it is the next player's turn to offer a touch.

5. When everyone outside the circle has had two turns, the person in the circle chooses someone else to be inside it.

6. Repeat until everyone has had a turn inside the circle. Always respect everyone's right to say "Yes" or "No."

Making Requests

When toddlers or preschoolers begin to talk, they start using words to ask for what they want or need. Some children try to get what they want by whining, begging, demanding, blaming, complaining, grabbing, or assuming. Children of all ages (and even adults) can benefit from practicing the skill of making requests when there is something they want or need from someone else. It is important for family members to learn appropriate, polite ways of requesting something from one another. Making requests can happen only after boundaries are noticed and respected.

A request is like an invitation. It can lead to one of two responses: "yes" or "no." For example, "May I have some of your candy?" is a request. The person being asked may not wish to share. This person's wishes should be respected. (What would you say if someone asked you, "May I use your car?")

When parents make a request of their child, it is not the same as giving a direction. (See chapter six, "Following Directions.") A common mistake is for a parent to ask, "Do you want to get your shoes on?" when it is time to go. The child hears this as a request and may say, "No." A direction is stated with more certainty, like this: "It's time to go. Here are your shoes to put on."

Play these games if you want family members to:

◆ Use a pleasant tone of voice to ask for what they want instead of whining or crying
◆ Turn complaints into requests

- Resort less to begging, demanding, or pleading to get what they want
- Ask politely for what they want instead of blaming others or saying, "It's not fair."
- Speak kindly to each other instead of ordering each other around
- Learn how to make polite requests even if the answer may be "no"
- Be able to say "no" to others to protect their personal space or belongings

Tips for Making Requests

- Pay close attention to the tone of voice that you use in making requests. Model a cheerful tone so the person making a request can hear how to do it correctly.
- Give the requested item or favor when you hear a polite tone of voice. Sometimes this takes practice. Wait until the child tries again politely before giving the requested item.
- Even if the answer is going to be "no," the request still needs to be made politely. In the making requests games, the answer is typically "yes" in order to encourage the correct form for making requests. You can practice taking "no" for an answer later.
- Use the phrase "Do you have a request?" whenever you hear whining or complaining. For a very young child who whines, just model the correct way of requesting, along with the correct tone of voice. Use simple words like "please," or "juice, please." Then, when the child imitates the correct form of request, give him or her what was requested. This will encourage polite requests. Once your child has learned how to make polite requests, you can teach taking "no" for an answer.

9 *Ask Me*

Making Requests

Play game 9 to practice the appropriate words and tone of voice to use when making a request.

Set-up

Space to play
Apple or other interesting item

Directions

1. Sit in a circle.

2. Choose one family member to start. This person holds an apple and turns to look at the person on her left.

3. The person on the left requests the apple.

The person holding the apple listens to the request.

4. If the request was stated in an acceptable way, she gives the apple to the person.

5. If the request was not satisfactory—for example, whining, demanding, or spoken too softly to be heard—then the person holding the apple models a better way to ask, including tone of voice.

6. The requesting person tries again until the giver of the apple is satisfied with the request and gives the apple. Now it is the new apple holder's turn to listen to a request from the next person on his left.

7. Continue until the apple has made its way around the circle.

8. To play again, switch places so that different family members are making requests of one another. Vary the object players are asking for.

10 My Request Card

Making Requests

Play game 10 to practice making polite requests of all members of the family, even though the answer may be "no."

Set-up

Space to play

Small treasures such as balloons, feathers, small toys, costume jewelry, key chains, knickknacks, etc. These items should be reserved for this game and not belong to any of the children in the family.

One bag for the treasures and one empty bag

Index cards or paper cut into 3" x 5" pieces, one for each player

Pen or marker

Prizes, such as a small bag of chips, a special drink, a storybook to read to a child, etc.

Directions

1. Sit in a circle

2. Choose someone to begin. Give her a "request card" and the empty bag.

3. Each other family member takes two items from the treasure bag and holds them.

4. The child with the request card turns to the person on her left and politely asks for one of the items that person is holding.

5. If the person asked feels that the request was made politely, then he says, "Thank

you for asking so nicely," and initials one of the boxes on her request card. Then he answers in one of two ways: "Yes, you may have the [item]," and gives the item to the requester; or "No, you may not have the [item]."

6. The child with the request card then asks the next person for a treasure, and continues asking until her card is filled with initials. She may then trade the card for a prize.

7. All the treasures are put back into the treasure bag, and someone else is chosen to have a turn with a request card.

8. Continue the game until everyone has had a turn making requests and has filled their cards.

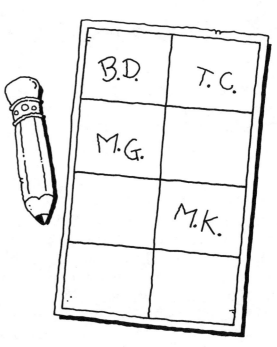

11 Mix and Match

Making Requests

Play game 11 to practice making requests and practice saying either "yes" or "no" in response.

Set-up

Space to play

One small basket or container for each family member.

One set of six matching objects for each player. Example: six red balls, six blue blocks, six small cars, six building blocks, six seashells, etc. (For older children, you can make six cards for each person out of different colors of construction paper. Or, you can pick up six each of different colors of fuzzy balls in the cat toy department of a pet store, having one set of six balls for each person in the family.)

Directions

1. Mix up the items and place a mixed collection in a basket or container for each player.

2. Sit in a circle.

3. Each person decides in advance on an item he or she will collect. Let the youngest family member decide first, then the next youngest, and so on.

4. Give each person a basket of mixed items.

5. A parent begins by asking any other player, "[Name], may I have one of your [item]?"

6. The person may answer "Yes" or "No." If "yes," then she gives the parent the item requested.

7. The person to the left of the parent is the next player to request the item he has decided on.

8. Continue playing the game until each player has obtained the complete set of items he or she has decided on.

Variation: Instead of telling in advance which item you will collect, keep it a secret until you are ready to ask for it. You may also change your mind while you are collecting one item and decide to collect a different item.

12 *Hands Off!*

Making Requests

Play game 12 to help children remember to make requests before touching other people's property, even if what they want to touch is not near the person it belongs to.

Set-up

Table and chairs
Timer
Blank removable stickers (labels) or masking tape and a marker
Collection of items, three for each player: a variety of toys, costume jewelry, feathers, beanbags, deck of cards, etc. Avoid using items that belong to any of the children in the family.

Directions

1. Sit around the table.

2. Place all the treasures in the middle of the table.

3. The first player chooses one item from the pile.

4. Mark the item with a sticker or a piece of tape that has her name on it.

5. After the first player chooses, then the next player on the left chooses, etc.

6. Once everyone has had a turn to choose an item, go around the table again and have each player pick a second item, and so on, until all the items belong (for the

duration of the game) to someone. Label each item with the taker's name.

7. Each player takes her own items and places them in different spots in the room.

8. Set the timer for three minutes.

9. All family members wander through the room, making a request to touch or look at items that belong to someone else. Players may answer "yes" or "no."

10. Play until the bell rings, then decide if you want to play again.

Listening

As children become more sociable in their preschool and kindergarten years, they need to learn how to pay attention to the needs and feelings of others. By learning the skill of listening, they will discover that other people have feelings, thoughts, and opinions that differ from their own. This is an important discovery that will help lay the groundwork for developing skills for getting along with others.

The skill of listening involves showing or telling another person that you understand what they want or how they feel. For a very young child, listening means paying attention to what the other person wants. As children get older, they can learn to listen for another person's feelings, opinions, wishes, and desires.

Listening to what someone wants does not mean you will grant his wishes. It just means you understand what he wants. For example, you can listen to your preschooler when he says, "I want a cookie," right before dinner. You can say, "Sounds like you're hungry." You may not give him a cookie, but you may give him choices on how to cope with the situation. For example, "Dinner will be in five minutes. While you're waiting, do you want to help me set the table, or do you want to keep playing?" If he cries, you can allow that, too. You can say, "Sounds like you're upset you can't have the cookie. You can cry if you want to, or you can help me set the timer for five minutes so you'll know when it's time to eat. When the bell rings, you can eat your dinner."

It is important for a child to feel his wishes and points of view are valid and acceptable. If he feels that his feelings and wishes are not heard and understood, then he may act them out in his behavior, maybe appearing stubborn, aggressive, moody, sullen, inflexible, or demanding. Sometimes you can listen effectively, and your child will still act out. This is because he is unhappy about not getting what he wants. Practice the taking "no" for an answer games (chapter five) and do not give him what he wants when he is acting out.

Play these games if you want family members to:

- Listen to other people's ideas
- Be more aware of the feelings and wishes of others
- Have a chance to speak their minds or give their opinions
- Feel like their ideas and feelings are valued by other family members
- Wait until someone is finished speaking before interrupting or finishing their sentences for them
- Give others a chance to have their say, or to have things go their way
- Pay attention to someone whose feelings or opinions may often be overlooked

Tips for Listening

- Pay attention to a person's facial expression and behavior. The skill of listening means more than just listening to what someone says. For example, if someone slams a door, it might be an expression of anger or frustration. If you just keep saying, "Don't slam the door!" you may miss an opportunity to be a good listener who helps someone cope with strong feelings and find solutions to his or her problems.
- If a child says, "I hate you," or swears at you, your immediate reaction might be to discipline her, or tell her not to talk like that. Instead, try listening: "Wow, sounds like you're really mad about something. I'd like to know about it." This can open the door to a conversation that may address the root of the problem, so that it can be solved. If you are too quick to discipline her for how she is telling you something, you may miss the opportunity to help her cope with her strong feelings.
- Teach children to use listening skills with you and with each other. Children are more likely to offer their respect when they understand your point of

view, rather than doing what you want just because you "say so."

- When you discipline your child, ask yourself, "What is my child learning from this?" If you listen carefully, you will find out through your child's words and behavior what she or he has learned. Is it what you intended? For example, if your child is sent to his room or grounded for misbehavior, is he likely to be more secretive in the future so as not to get caught? Is this what you hoped he would learn?

13 My Echo

Listening

Play game 13 to encourage brothers and sisters to respect one another by listening to each other's ideas and to ask before grabbing.

Set-up

Space to play
Hula Hoop® or masking tape
Two beanbags (or rolled-up pairs of socks)
Basket or box
Paper bag
Foam ball
Jump rope
(Next time you play, use different items.)

Directions

1. Place the Hula Hoop® on the floor or make a circle of tape on the floor and put all the props inside the circle.

2. Choose a child to invent a family game using some or all of the props in the circle and to show others how to play the game.

3. Choose a second child to listen to the idea and to repeat it to the first child.

4. The child inventing the game may want to try out the items, or use them to demonstrate his idea. Before touching any item in the circle to demonstrate, he must first ask permission from all the others to get the item (or items) out of the hoop.

For example, "May I take the rope and the beanbag to show you something?"

5. Each of the other players in turn must say "yes" before he takes the item from the circle.

If a brother or sister does not say "yes," this withholding indicates a competition for attention. See if the child inventing the game can get the naysayer to say "yes." The child who is asking can use this opportunity to listen to the withholder.

6. Then the child takes the items and shows and tells the family how to use them in the game.

7. The second child (#3 above) listens and repeats the instructions.

8. When the inventor feels that his idea was understood as repeated to him, the family plays the game as it was described and demonstrated.

9. Then it is the next child's turn to describe her idea. Continue until each child has:

   a. had a turn inventing a game and

   b. repeating a game's instructions verbally before you play it.

14 *My Favorite Things*

Listening

Play game 14 to help family members pay attention to and remember the feelings and wishes of others.

Set-up

Table and chairs

Miscellaneous items (at least two for each person in the family), such as: several toys, deck of cards, one or two pieces of costume jewelry, food items (fruit, can of juice, container of yogurt), etc.

Directions

1. Place all the items on the table and sit in chairs around the table.

2. A parent decides who will go first, and play proceeds to the left.

3. The first player looks at all the items, and says:

   "My favorite is the [item] because [reason]."

   (For example, "My favorite is the pink necklace because pink is my favorite color.")

4. Then the next player describes one favorite item. Continue until all players have had a turn describing their favorite things.

5. The first player now takes a second turn. This time, she picks another family

member, and recalls what his or her favorite item was and why. (For example, "Mom's favorite was the strawberry yogurt because she thinks it tastes so good.")

6. The next player on the left picks a different family member and describes that person's favorite thing, and so on. Go around the table until everyone has described the favorite item of someone else.

7. Repeat the game, everyone telling a second favorite item. On the second round, each player recalls both the first and the second favorite item of another family member.

15 *Look at Me*

Listening

Play game 15 to help children learn to notice feelings of others by "reading" their faces.

Set-up

Table and chairs
Paper
Colored marker

Directions

1. Using a marker, divide a piece of paper into four parts. In each section, draw one of four feeling pictures: happy face, mad face, sad face, and scared face.

2. All players sit around the table. A parent chooses someone to go first.

3. The first player makes a face that shows one of the four feelings on the paper.

4. Other players raise their hand if they know what the feeling is. The first player chooses someone to guess.

5. If that person guesses correctly, then he gets the next turn.

6. Continue until everyone has had at least two chances to guess the feeling.

7. Once these four basic feelings are mastered, try the game without using the drawings. Older children can read more subtle feelings and expressions.

16 Hey, You–Catch!

Listening

Play game 16 to practice getting the attention of your listener.

Set-up

Space to play
One pair of rolled-up socks for each person
Timer

Directions

1. Sit in a circle.

2. Set the timer for three minutes.

3. Parent says the name of one of the other players. Wait until he is paying attention and then throw the sock ball to him.

4. The catcher says the name of someone else, and tosses the sock ball as soon as that person is paying attention.

5. Meanwhile, the parent who began the game takes a second sock ball and chooses someone else to toss it to.

6. Keep the game going, with the parent adding more sock balls until the bell rings.

7. Collect the sock balls. Play the game again.

Note: This game is wonderfully chaotic with everyone tossing balls at the same time. The trick is to listen for your name and be ready to catch a ball, and to be sure that the person you are tossing to is ready to catch your ball.

Taking "No" for an Answer

In many families, children have trouble taking "no" for an answer. Instead, they whine, cry, beg, plead, argue, manipulate, sulk, throw tantrums, hit, or do what they please anyway. They think this behavior will change their parents' minds. Sometimes it does. This pay-off teaches them to continue with such unpleasant behaviors.

Getting "no" for an answer may lead to feelings of frustration, anger, or disappointment. These feelings are powerful human emotions. We all need to learn to cope with them. If we are frustrated or angry, we need to learn how to calm ourselves down and regain our composure. If we feel hurt or disappointed, we need to learn how to comfort ourselves. Practicing taking "no" for an answer can help children cope with these kinds of feelings.

First, children need to learn how to make requests. (See chapter three, "Making Requests.") When you make a request, you might get an answer of "yes," or you might get "no." That is the nature of a request. Children may think that if they state a request in a polite way, they deserve a "yes" answer. It is important for children to practice making requests that lead to a "no" answer as well.

We need to teach children to make polite requests first, regardless of whether the answer will be "yes" or "no." Suppose it's right before supper-time, and your child whines for a cookie. Instead of saying, "No, it's just before supper," say, "Do you have a request?" Then model the words and tone of voice you want to hear: "May I please have a cookie?" If your child makes a polite request, you are not obliged to say "yes" to reward the politeness! Thank her for asking so politely and then give your answer. Do this even if you know all along that the answer will be "no."

As parents, we can teach our children to ask politely for what they want (making requests) and at the same time teach them to accept "no."

Play these games if you want family members to:

- Learn that hitting, crying, whining, arguing, begging, pleading, or bartering will not turn a "no" into a "yes"
- Listen to you instead of ignoring you when you say "no"
- Learn how to cope with feeling frustrated, angry, or disappointed
- Give clear answers instead of being unsure and saying, "maybe," or "we'll see"
- Be able to say "no" even if someone might have a negative reaction, instead of being afraid of his reaction
- Learn how to stop, even when he is excited or upset
- Learn how to stop immediately when you ask someone to stop doing something that is irritating

Tips for Taking "No" for an Answer

- Ignore (do not comment on) your child's whining, begging, arguing, complaining, or attempting to take over. Instead, just carry on with the game. If your child persists, you can say, "I bet you think I'll change my mind if you whine [hit, cry]. Well, I won't."
- Respect your child's right to say "no" to requests.
- If one member of the family always says "no" when a request is made of him or her, your family may need more practice in listening. (See chapter four, "Listening.") Or you may need to seek professional advice if you keep encountering oppositional behavior.
- Help your child distinguish between a request and a direction. Do this by telling him in advance: " I have a request"; or "This is not a request, this is a direction. I need you to follow directions exactly." (See chapter six, "Following Directions.")

17 *May I Have Your Seat, Please?*

Taking "No" for an Answer

Play game 17 to practice taking "no" for an answer when making a request.

Set-up

Space to play
Pillows or chairs for each person to sit on or in
Timer
Beanbag or rolled-up pair of socks

Directions

1. Set the timer for five minutes.

2. Everyone sits in a circle on a pillow or in a chair.

3. One person holds a beanbag. This person stands up, approaches another family member, and says, "May I have your seat, please?" The person asked may answer "yes" or "no."

4. If the answer is "no," the person making the request asks someone else.

5. If the answer is "yes," then the person making the request hands the beanbag to the person who said "yes," and sits down in her chair. Now it is that person's turn to ask the same question of other players.

6. Continue until the timer rings.

18 Traffic Cop

Taking "No" for an Answer

Play game 18 to practice stopping.

Set-up

Space to play

Chair for the traffic cop, placed in the middle of the room or off to one side

STOP sign made out of paper or cardboard and colored red

Directions

1. Choose a child to be the traffic cop. This child sits in the chair and holds the STOP sign in her lap.

2. Pick another player to be the "traffic." Everyone else watches at this point.

3. When the traffic cop says "go," the traffic moves around the room, clapping loudly. She or he must keep an eye on the traffic cop.

4. When the traffic cop holds up the STOP sign, the traffic must stop immediately and stand quietly in place. If the traffic has trouble stopping right away, keep practicing until he or she can.

5. Pick a second person to be "traffic." This time both players move around and clap loudly when the traffic cop says "go." When they see the STOP sign go up, they both stop immediately.

6. Pick yet another person to add to the traffic and repeat the game as above. Keep adding traffic until all family members are playing. Everyone must keep an eye on the traffic cop.

7. Continue playing for three minutes.

8. Pick someone else to be the traffic cop and play again. Vary the activity of the traffic: sing, stomp, dance, make traffic noises, etc.

Note: Sometimes it is hard for children to stop, so this game gives them practice. Stopping instantly is a skill young children, especially, need in order to avoid danger. Another benefit is that the child who is the traffic cop gets to feel powerful, and this feeling builds self-esteem.

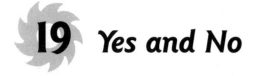

19 Yes and No

Taking "No" for an Answer

Play game 19 to help children practice dealing with frustration.

Set-up

Space to play

Container (basket, bowl, or box) for each player

Miscellaneous items that do not belong to children in the family (toys, balls, feathers, costume jewelry, etc.)

Feelings chart

Directions

1. A parent chooses someone to be the petitioner, who will ask for items.

2. Other family members are given a collection of items to put in their containers.

3. The petitioner is given an empty container in which to put the items she collects.

4. Set the timer for one minute.

5. The petitioner begins by requesting one item at a time from any other player.

6. On the first round, everyone says "Yes" and gives her the item she has asked for.

7. On the second round, set the timer again for one minute. This time everyone says "No."

8. When the timer rings, the petitioner looks at the feelings chart and identifies the picture that matches how she feels.

9. On the third round, set the timer for one minute. This time each player decides whether to say "Yes" or "No." If "yes," she is given the item.

10. Repeat step eight.

11. Then it is the next child's turn for three rounds.

Note: Help children find ways to cope with strong feelings. When they feel mad, they can count to ten to calm down. When they feel sad, they can take three deep breaths to comfort themselves. If they feel like giving up, next time they might keep trying instead, or ask for help. If they feel they want to keep trying, praise them. Persistence is a helpful trait.

They also might want to practice backing off, because extreme persistence can annoy others.

Variation: Assign different family members to say all "yes," all "no," or a combination of the two.

Feelings Chart

20 Hopovers

Taking "No" for an Answer

Play game 20 to practice feeling what it is like to be told "yes" and "no."

Set-up

Space to play
Masking tape

Directions

1. Place a line of masking tape across the floor in the middle of the room.

2. Pick a player to be the leader and have her stand behind the line.

3. Other players stand in front of the line.

4. One of them asks the leader, "May I hop over to your side?" If the leader says, "Yes, you may," the player hops over the line to join her. If the leader says, "No, you may not," the player sits down where he is.

5. Play continues in this manner until all the players have had a turn to ask to join the leader.

6. The leader then says, "You all did a great job of asking. Some of you also did a great job of taking 'no' for an answer."

7. Pick another player to be the leader and play again.

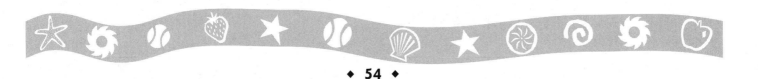

21 *Invisible Leader*

Taking "No" for an Answer

Play game 21 to help children practice coping with being left out.

Set-up

Space to play
Timer

Directions

1. Pick one child to be the leader.

2. Set the timer for one minute.

3. Everyone in the family ignores the leader completely until the timer rings. During this time the leader finds a way to occupy himself.

4. As soon as the timer rings, set it again for one minute.

5. Everyone pays attention to the leader during this minute.

6. Pick another child to be the leader, and set the timer again.

7. Repeat until each child has had a turn first being ignored and then getting attention.

Note: Talk about what it feels like to be ignored or left out and what it is like to be the center of attention. When people are not paying attention to you, it does not mean they do not like you. What can a child do to feel okay, even when he or she is not the center of attention? Make a list with your child.

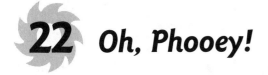

22 *Oh, Phooey!*

Taking "No" for an Answer

Play game 22 to help children practice coping with not getting exactly what they want.

Set-up

Space to sit in a circle on the floor or at a table
Masking tape or Hula Hoop®
Items that people in the family like: toys, food, etc. You need two more items than family members.

Directions

1. Place the items in the center of a circle of tape or inside the Hula Hoop®.

2. Sit around the circle or the Hula Hoop®.

3. Pick someone to be the leader.

4. The leader asks each person in turn, "Which thing is your favorite?"

5. After everyone has named a favorite item, the leader gives something to each family member, not giving any favored item to the person who wanted it.

6. Family members practice coping with disappointment by saying, "Thanks for the [item]. I would have preferred to get the [item]. Next time, could I please have the [favored item]?"

7. Pick a new leader and play again, this time giving some people what they want and not others.

8. Repeat step 6.

Following Directions

From toddlers to teens, children have a tendency to want to do things in their own way. Learning the skill of following directions exactly will help them be more successful both in their relationships and in their life achievements.

It is important for all family members to be able to follow rules and directions. When a family member rebels against following rules or directions, things do not go smoothly in the family, and angry interactions usually result. Children need to follow parents' directions, because parents are acting as their guides to life. However, directions given or rules set by parents need to be relevant and consistent.

Parents will be more successful when they learn the difference between giving directions and making requests. When a request is made of someone, it is like an invitation. The other person has the genuine option of saying "yes" or saying "no" to decline the request. When a parent gives a child a direction to follow, the parent expects the child to take the described action, and follows through to make sure the action is taken. This is not a request.

In healthy families, parents are in charge. This means that the parents are running the family, and not the children. It is important for children to follow parents' directions. Parents, in turn, show respect for their children's leadership abilities by allowing them to be the ones who give directions at times, within limits set by the parents.

Play these games if you want family members to:

◆ Listen to your directions
◆ Do what you ask the first time
◆ Do chores without arguing
◆ Complete a job correctly the first time
◆ Learn to pay attention to directions given without words (with gestures)
◆ Learn to be a good leader and a good follower
◆ Behave the way you want them to when you are out in public
◆ Feel important and powerful while at the same time allowing parents to be in charge

Tips for Following Directions

◆ Keep the mood of the game upbeat and positive.
◆ Give directions in a calm, pleasant tone of voice. Avoid scolding, criticizing, nagging, or complaining about how the player follows (or doesn't follow) the directions.
◆ If directions are not followed exactly, have the player try again until he or she gets it right. Even very young children should not be let off the hook: make sure their performance is exact. Simplify directions if necessary to ensure a young child's success. Make directions more complex to challenge a child who finds them too easy.
◆ Pass play on to another family member if someone refuses to follow directions or follows them incorrectly deliberately. Do not scold or coax resistant players.
◆ Pay attention to cooperative behavior, and ignore resistant or oppositional behavior.
◆ Cheer on each player with enthusiasm. Say things like: "Way to go!" "Great job following directions!" "You did it exactly!"

23 *Follow the Leader*

Following Directions
Play game 23 to establish parents (adults) as leaders in the family.

Set-up
Space to play
Timer

Directions
1. Set the timer for five minutes.

2. A parent is in charge. This parent picks someone in the family to be the leader in a game of "Follow the Leader." (The parent can pick him- or herself, too.)

3. The chosen leader does various positions, movements, and/or facial expressions for others to copy.

4. After about 10 to 30 seconds, the parent in charge interrupts the first leader, and picks someone else to be the leader.

5. After another 10 to 30 seconds, the parent picks someone else, and so on.

6. The parent continues choosing different leaders until the timer rings.

24 *I Got It!*

Following Directions

Play game 24 to help children practice following directions exactly as they are given.

Set-up

Space to play
List of directions

Directions

1. Sit in chairs or on the floor in a circle.

2. Pick one child to start.

3. This child stands in the middle of the circle and waits for directions.

4. Give the child a direction from the sample list.

5. After the child follows the first direction exactly, the next family member in the circle has a turn to give her a direction.

6. Continue until everyone sitting in the circle has had a turn to *give* a direction.

7. A parent then chooses another child to stand in the middle and follow directions (from the list or make up your own).

List of Directions

Touch your toes.

Turn around three times.

Go and touch the door and then come back to me.

Clap your hands while I count to ten, then stop.

Stand on one foot and count to five.

Sit in that chair, count to seven aloud, and then come back to me.

Recite the alphabet from A to Z.

Tell your full name and phone number.

Count backwards from ten to one.

Stomp your feet, clap your hands, and say, "Hip, Hip, Hooray!"

Note: You can make up more challenging directions for older children.

25 *Pantomime Game*

Following Directions
Play game 25 to practice giving and following non-verbal directions.

Set-up
Space to play
Places to sit (chairs, couches, pillows, etc.)

Directions
1. Sit in a circle on the floor or in chairs.

2. Choose one family member to be the leader.

3. This person stands up, turns to someone in the family, and uses invented sign language to direct that person to go and sit in another chair or spot in the room.

4. The leader does not touch the person and does not use any words.

5. After the leader has finished directing each of the other family members, he then picks someone else to have a turn as leader.

6. Continue until everyone has had a turn using gestures to direct the others.

26 *Follow Me, Follow You*

Following Directions

Play game 26 to practice being both leader and follower.

Set-up

Space to play
Timer or bell
Scarf or small towel

Directions

1. Pick two family members to start: one is the leader and the other is the follower.

2. The leader holds one end of the scarf or towel, and the follower holds the other end.

3. A third family member rings the bell or timer.

4. The leader leads the follower all around the room. (The follower may be blindfolded to increase the challenge level.)

5. After 10 to 20 seconds, the timer or bell is rung again. The players reverse roles.

6. Repeat step five several times (four or five).

7. Pick another two family members.

8. Repeat the game until all pairs in the family have had a turn. If you have an uneven number of people in your family, someone may need to play more than once.

Acknowledging Others

Acknowledging other people means that you recognize and respond to them for who they are and what they do. It is also an expression of thanks or appreciation. Being acknowledged makes people feel important. They can see that their actions, or even just their presence, makes a difference to others.

Children tend to be mostly self-centered until they are around seven or eight years old. Until then, it is hard for them to see things from another person's point of view. Even if they are too young to empathize with others, they can still learn the skill of acknowledging. When children and teens are able to indicate appreciation and thanks to oth-ers, they will have more satisfying relationships.

The skill of acknowledging others means that you say (aloud and without judgment) that you notice another person's feelings, opinions, or actions. For example, "Your mouth is turned down. I wonder if you're sad"; "You like the red one"; or "You slammed the door really hard."

Acknowledgment includes praise, but not the kind of praise that judges or evaluates, such as, "You are a good girl." If a child hears such praise often, she may become dependent on the approval of others and anxious to avoid disapproval. Praise is more effective when you describe what you see and how it affects you. Instead of saying, "What a good helper you are," you can say, "You carried it all the way across the room, and it was heavy! Now I don't have to do it myself." When you make this kind of statement, your child can draw her own conclusions about what kind of person she is (in this case, strong and helpful). Factual observations give a child power to choose to act in ways that will benefit others because she knows *what she did* that was helpful.

Acknowledging others can also be thanking or telling them what you appreciate about them.

Play these games if you want family members to:

◆ Get along well with one another
◆ Say kind things to or about each other, instead of being mean
◆ Notice one another in positive ways
◆ Find things they like about each other, instead of focusing on what they do not like
◆ Feel appreciated and valued
◆ Feel recognized for their efforts
◆ Talk to each other, instead of ignoring or avoiding one another
◆ Be motivated to please one another and to do things the way others like them done

Tips for Acknowledging Others

◆ Make sure the least or less favorite family members get acknowledged, too. Families often have favorite members who are easy to acknowledge, and the others get left out in the cold.
◆ For those who have trouble thinking of an appreciation or acknowledgment, give them extra time, or give them the homework of bringing two acknowledgments to the next day's game.
◆ Incorporate these games into your daily routine. For example, play them each evening at the dinner table. Make acknowledging a family habit.
◆ Pay attention to how each family member receives acknowledgment. It is important for children and adults to be able to accept compliments and praise from others graciously.
◆ Remember to avoid using praise that evaluates a child. Stay away from words like good, thoughtful, strong. Instead, describe the outcome, or its effect on you. "It saved me a lot of trouble"; "It made me feel good inside"; "That was a very heavy box you carried."

27 *Hello, There!*

Acknowledging Others

Play game 27 to help children practice greeting someone and remembering that people need to be greeted.

Set-up

Space to play
Timer
Foam ball or other soft ball
Beanbag
Small pillow

Directions

1. Sit in a circle.

2. Place the props nearby. Start with the foam ball.

3. Set the timer for one minute.

4. A parent goes first. This parent says to a family member, "Hello, [name]," and tosses the ball to that person.

5. Then the receiver chooses someone else in the family, and says, "Hello [name]," and tosses the ball to her.

6. Continue the tossing until the bell rings.

7. When the bell rings, switch to a different prop, and re-set the timer for one minute.

8. Continue switching props each time the timer rings, until all the props have been used.

28 Compliments

Acknowledging Others

Play game 28 to practice giving and receiving compliments and to add the word "compliment" to your child's vocabulary.

Set-up

Space to play

Directions

1. Sit in a circle in chairs or on the floor.

2. Pick someone to go first.

3. This person gives a compliment to each other family member in turn. Examples of compliments are: "That color looks nice on you," "I like your haircut," "You play the piano beautifully," etc.

4. Each person receiving a compliment says, "Thank you" in a pleasant tone.

5. Then the next player to the left has a turn to give a compliment to each other player.

6. Keep playing until everyone has had a turn giving a compliment and receiving one graciously.

29 *Wish Me a Rainbow*

Acknowledging Others
Play game 29 to practice paying attention to each other's dreams and wishes.

Set-up
Space to play

Directions
1. Sit in a circle on the floor or in chairs around a table.

2. A parent goes first. This parent looks at another family member, and says, "[Name], I bet you wish _____." The parent fills in the blank by mentioning one thing that person would like. For example, "[Name], I bet you wish to eat a big juicy mango." [Or go to Disneyworld; or get a new guitar; etc.] "Am I right?" If the child says "No," ask her to state one thing she would like.

3. Then it is the child's turn to choose someone else, and say, "[Name], I bet you wish _____. Am I right?"

4. Continue until everyone has had several turns to say, "I bet you wish . . ." and to have their wishes acknowledged by being asked, "Am I right?"

30 *Circle of Thanks*

Acknowledging Others

Play game 30 daily to encourage positive interactions and good feelings among family members.

Set-up

Space to play

Directions

1. Sit in a circle on the floor or around a table.

2. Pick someone to go first.

3. This person looks at the person on his left, and says: "I want to thank you for _____." (Think of something this person did recently or in the past.)

4. Then he turns to the next family member in the circle and thanks her for something.

5. He keeps going around the circle until he has said something to every other person in the family.

6. The person on his left goes next.

7. Continue playing the game until everyone has had a turn thanking each other family member.

8. Repeat the game, this time saying: "I appreciate it when you _____." (Think of something the person does that you like.)

Planning

The skill of planning is essential for helping families make it through their days, weeks, and weekends. It also helps family members cope with new or unexpected events. When all family members are involved in the planning, they are more likely to agree to the plan, and to cooperate rather than resisting or complaining, even if the subject is chores! Plans can help family members know what is going to happen next, so that they can increase their confidence and their level of cooperation.

Play these games if you want family members to:

- Spend time together
- Do new activities together
- Do chores, and maybe even enjoy them
- Cooperate quickly when it is time to change from one activity to another
- Entertain themselves without interrupting when you are on the phone or talking to one another
- Have a chance to be the center of attention once in a while
- Wait patiently while you finish an errand or conversation
- Spend time with a family member they do not often spend time with

Tips for Planning

- Write plans down. Use pictures, drawings, diagrams, or photos of activities for children who are not yet reading.
- Record each family member's activities or events on a calendar. Every day, check the calendar

and put a line through the previous day. Every week, write in the next week's activities. Use a different color to represent each person's activities.

◆ Record a planned event or appointment on the calendar in advance with your child's help. Use the scheduling time to describe in detail what your child can expect, which will help diffuse objections and worries if the event is not necessarily pleasant (dental appointment, for example). Use words or drawings to write a story about what will happen.

◆ Practice planning every day.

◆ Allow time for spontaneous activities, too.

31 *What Shall We Do Next?*

Planning

Play game 31 to practice making a schedule to prepare for what to do next, and to prevent power struggles when it is time to move on to another activity or routine.

Set-up

Place to sit, preferably at a table
Paper
Marker or pen
Optional: chalkboard and chalk, or whiteboard and markers

Directions

1. Before setting up to play this game, select the games you want to play from this book and write the names down in the order you will play them today.

2. Sit with family members around the table.

3. Place the paper on the table or the board nearby where everyone can see it.

4. Draw a small square after each game.

5. Write number one beside the first game you will play, number two beside the second one, and so on.

6. Add a line at the end of the games for a favored activity, such as the opportunity to play with certain items or to eat certain snacks. Put a number next to this activity as well. It will be the last one on the list.

7. Look at the schedule and point to what you are going to do first. Play game number one. Ask a child to place a check mark in the square next to number one when that activity is finished.

8. Look at the schedule to see what game is next. Continue until all the games have been played and checked off. If anyone objects to the order, just say you are following the schedule (no one can argue with a piece of paper or a chalkboard).

Yum Yum	☑ 1
Captain May I	☐ 4
Hands Off	☐ 2
Traffic Cop	☐ 3
Have Dessert!	☐ 5

32 *My Time*

Planning

Play game 32 to avoid problems with children who interrupt and seek attention when parents are busy.

Set-up

Two chairs
Masking tape
Timer
Paper and markers
Optional: whiteboard and markers, or chalkboard and chalk
Several containers of small toys, games, cards, or drawing materials

Directions

1. Use masking tape to mark a boundary around the two chairs where parents will be sitting, facing one another. If only one parent is playing, he or she can sit inside the boundary holding the telephone, pretending to talk to someone.

2. Make a schedule on the paper or the board that looks like this:

	Child #1	Child #2	Child #3
1ST Two Minutes			
2ND Two Minutes			
3rd Two Minutes			

3. Set the containers of items on the floor.

4. Pick one child to start planning. This child looks at all the items and decides how she will spend the times when her parent is busy.

5. She picks out an activity to do during the first two minutes, one for the second two minutes, and one for the third (last) two minutes.

6. Write her choices in the appropriate boxes on the schedule. Draw the activity if your child is too young to read.

7. Pick another child to make his plan the same way. He can include in his plan any materials that are not going to be used by another child at the same time.

8. Continue until all your children have their parts of the schedule filled in.

9. Set the timer for two minutes.

10. Parents talk to one another and ignore the children while they each play with the activity they chose. (Or one parent talks on the phone and ignores the children.)

11. When the timer goes off, the children can refer to the chart to see which activity comes next. (At first, parents may need to help children refer to the chart when the timer rings. With practice, they can do this independently.)

12. Set the timer for two more minutes. Repeat number ten.

13. Repeat number nine and ten.

14. At the end of the six minutes, pay attention to the children and thank them for playing without interrupting you.

33 Chore Partners

Planning

Play game 33 to encourage a positive attitude about doing chores and to encourage family interactions.

Set-up

Space to sit at the table
Paper and pencil

Directions

1. All family members sit at the table.

2. Make a list of chores that need to be done (same number of chores as people in the family). Draw pictures to represent the chores for young children who cannot read. Examples: clean the floor of the front closet, wash the dog, sweep the patio, vacuum the hall, wash the bathroom mirror, etc.

3. Read the list of chores aloud.

4. Give the youngest child first choice to pick a chore. Then the next youngest picks, and so on. Write each person's name opposite the chore he chose.

5. For each chore, a team of two people is needed. The youngest child can choose a partner, or the parent can assign a partner. Write down the second name next to each of the chores on the list.

6. Each person will have two chores to do, and each team should have different partners, if possible.

7. Set the timer for ten minutes. Put on some lively music and get to work!

8. When the timer rings, check in with everyone to see how much they have done. Reset the timer and keep going. As teams finish the first chore, they re-form into the second team and begin their second chore. Some partners may have to wait a bit until their new partner is ready.

9. At first, keep this game short, no longer than 20 or 30 minutes. The idea is that everyone should feel good about working together to accomplish a goal. Later you can decide to do more chores during this game.

10. After you have finished, celebrate what you accomplished together in some enjoyable manner.

Making and Keeping Agreements

Family members need to know they can count on one another to follow through with their agreements. Children who can keep agreements are showing that they can be responsible. When they show that they are responsible, then they can be given more freedom and privileges. Making and keeping agreements is a skill that family members need to practice.

Sometimes, a family member may find excuses for breaking an agreement made earlier. Rather than falling into a pattern of broken agreements and excuses, teach children how to renegotiate before the fact. For example, what if a special family friend drops by just as bedtime comes at 8:30 pm? A responsible child will approach his parents, saying, "May I make an agreement to go to bed at 9:00 tonight instead of 8:30? Then I can visit with Uncle Joe."

Play these games if you want family members to:

◆ Be on time
◆ Report back or call home at exactly the time they said they would
◆ Keep you informed at all times about where they are
◆ Keep promises instead of disappointing one another, or making excuses
◆ Do what they said they would, when they said they would
◆ Do chores without reminders
◆ Follow the rules without arguing

◆ 79 ◆

Tips for Making and Keeping Agreements

- It is important to learn to keep agreements even though you may not want to.
- It may help to write agreements down, and then check them off when the agreement is completed. This will help family members remember what they agreed to do.
- It is important for family members to keep their word. This builds trust and demonstrates responsibility.
- If circumstances change, try to keep your agreement anyway. If you need to change your agreement, make sure you make a new agreement.
- Following rules of the house is a form of keeping agreements. If circumstances interfere with following a rule, make sure family members talk to each other to change the agreement. For example, the rule says the dishes need to be done right after dinner, but you have to leave for your child's piano recital. Make an agreement with each other before you leave to do the dishes as soon as you get back.

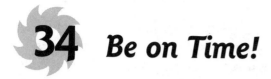

34 Be on Time!

Making and Keeping Agreements

Play game 34 to practice being on time as an important aspect of keeping agreements.

Set-up

Two rooms
Space to sit at the table
Two watches or clocks with a second hand
Note: Digital watches or clocks can also be used for this, but they do not show the passage of time like a sweep hand does.

Directions

1. Have everyone sit in chairs at the table.

2. A parent chooses one child to go first. This child puts on or holds a watch with a second hand. For a very young child's turn, use a clock, and teach him to watch the second hand going around. Place a mark at the top of the minute. Have him tell you when the second hand reaches the mark by shouting, "TIME!" In later turns, you can have him leave the room, taking the clock along, and return to his seat before the second hand gets to the top.

3. The child is asked to leave the room for one minute, and then to return on time.

Explain that "on time" means he is back at the table when the hand reaches the one-minute mark.

Someone at the table also has a watch or clock with a second hand to keep track of the time.

4. Take turns leaving the room and coming back on time.

5. Use different time intervals.

6. Experiment with having two people out at the same time, one for one minute, and the other for two minutes.

7. Cheer those who get back on time. If someone has trouble, have him practice again. A very young child may need an adult or older child as a partner in this game.

Note: In real life, use this method for a child to practice playing outside and coming back on time. Start with very short time periods, and as your child becomes more responsible, you can extend the times. Adults can play this game by being on time to pick up their children or meet their partners or get to appointments.

35 My Word

Making and Keeping Agreements
Play game 35 to help family members practice keeping their word.

Set-up
Several chairs and pillows on the floor, with twice as many seats as you have players
A bell or timer

Directions
1. Family members all sit in a seat of their choice to begin.

2. Each family member has a turn to say where he or she will go to sit next. For example, "I will sit over there on the blue chair." (Players may not choose a chair that is currently occupied or has been chosen by another player.)

3. Do not move yet! Wait until everyone chooses where they will go next.

4. A parent rings the bell, and everyone moves at the same time.

5. Check to make sure all players kept their agreement by going to the seat they said they would.

6. Repeat the game.

Note: Once you have practiced this game a few times, you may allow players to choose a chair that is occupied now, but will be empty when everyone moves to their new location.

36 *Helping Hands*

Making and Keeping Agreements

Play game 36 to practice keeping agreements about doing chores.

Set-up

Space to sit at a table
Paper and pencil

Directions

1. Everyone sits at the table.

2. Write on the paper a list of simple chores that need to be done. Write three more chores than there are family members.

3. Number each item on the list. For example, 1) sweep the kitchen floor, 2) gather up old newspapers, 3) fold the laundry, 4) dust the furniture in the living room

4. The youngest child picks out one of the chores first, saying, "I agree to dust the furniture in the living room."

5. Then the next youngest picks another chore, and so on, until everyone (including parents) has picked a chore and agreed to do it. Three chores will be left.

6. Do the chores, keeping your agreements. Afterwards, the whole family can celebrate with a special activity or treat.

Note: Make a daily schedule to encourage children to do chores regularly.

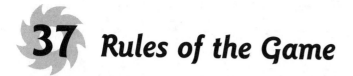

37 Rules of the Game

Making and Keeping Agreements

Play game 37 to help children practice following rules without arguing.

Set-up

Space to play
Paper
Marker or pen
Optional: whiteboard and markers, or chalkboard and chalk
Hula Hoop®
Pair of socks rolled into a ball
Paper bag
Scarf

Directions

1. Sit in chairs or on the floor in a circle.

2. Place the objects on the floor in the middle of the circle so everyone can see them.

3. Pick someone to go first. This player looks at the items and thinks up a rule for a game that could be played with them.

4. Write the rule on the whiteboard or on a piece of paper. Do not judge or correct the rule.

5. The next player on the left takes a turn looking at the items and thinks up another rule for the same game.

6. Continue until each family member has stated a rule for the game. Do not judge or correct any of the rules.

7. Play the game together, following all the rules exactly.

Note: Part of keeping agreements is doing exactly what was agreed without arguing or second guessing later.

Cooperating

Cooperating is an important skill that allows a feeling of "community" to develop in your family. When more people are involved in an activity, more can be accomplished than if you try to do something all by yourself. Cooperating means working together with others who may have different levels of skill or ability, or different points of view. How can you include everyone, even if their skill level is different from yours? Here, we learn the importance of tolerance for differences, which is the beginning of teamwork. Instead of competing and trying to be the first one or the best one, each child can learn to feel good about him- or herself as a member of a productive team. The skill of cooperating requires that all family members work together, taking into account various levels of ability and including everyone in the carrying out of an activity.

Play these games if you want family members to:

◆ Include one another even though abilities may differ

◆ Learn to tolerate and respect differences in ability, without having to be the best

◆ Allow someone else to be first now and then

◆ Be willing to try out other people's ideas

◆ Work together toward a common goal

◆ Participate and try their best, even when they are younger than others

◆ Appreciate and honor each other's skills and abilities

◆ Feel like a team

- Encourage cooperation instead of competition
- Have fun together

Tips for Cooperating

- Make sure all family members are included in the games. Make adjustments to accommodate different sizes or abilities.
- Stop or freeze play at times if needed to consider changes that might make the game more successful.
- Use some of the previous skills your family has practiced, like respecting boundaries, making requests, listening, taking "no" for an answer, following directions, acknowledging, planning, and making and keeping agreements.
- Notice if any of the previous skills need more practice.
- Think of other games your family can play using cooperating instead of competing.
- Modify the rules of some favorite games so that you are cooperating instead of competing.

38 *Sock Juggle*

Cooperating

Play game 38 to practice working together, while taking into account different skill levels.

Set-up

Space to play
Pair of rolled-up socks for each family member
Bag or basket to hold sock balls
Timer

Directions

Read instructions 1–7 aloud to your family, demonstrating the actions, before you begin to play the game.

1. Decide aloud in what order the first sock ball will be thrown to each person, starting with a parent. For example, Mom to younger brother to sister to Dad to older brother and back to Mom.

2. Toss the sock ball in the order decided above. The last person to catch it should be the parent who was first to throw it.

3. Repeat the same pattern of tossing. The same parent tosses to the same second person, who tosses to the same third person, etc.

4. Continue tossing until the sock ball is smoothly passed several times in the same pattern.

5. Then, the parent who started adds another

sock ball, and everyone keeps both sock balls going in the same pattern.

6. Add another one, and so on, until there are the same number of sock balls being passed as there are family members. Practice until all the sock balls can be successfully kept in motion.

7. Now that you have read all the instructions, set the timer for five minutes and begin with the first sock ball.

8. When the timer rings, decide together whether you want to play the game longer.

39 *Bouncing Beans*

Cooperating

Play game 39 to practice working together to achieve a common goal.

Set-up

Space to play
Scarf
Beanbag or a pair of rolled-up socks

Directions

1. Have all family members hold a corner or edge of the scarf.

2. Place a beanbag or sock ball in the center of the scarf.

3. Work together to bounce the beanbag or sock ball up in the air and catch it again in the scarf, as many times as you can.

4. Count how many times you can bounce the item and catch it before it falls to the ground.

5. Try again to see if you can better your score.

6. Set a target score for your family and stop when you reach it.

Note: If you play with sock balls, call this game "Soaring Socks."

40 Balloon Walk

Cooperating

Play game 40 to encourage family members to cooperate, even if they usually do not get along.

Set-up

Space to play
Masking tape
Six balloons or large balls
Laundry basket or large box
Watch or clock with a second hand
Paper and pencil or pen, to add scores

Note: The cover illustration shows this game.

Directions

1. Arrange the family into teams of two. If one person is left, this person is the time-keeper. If there is an even number of people in the family, choose someone in one of the teams to be the timekeeper, too.

2. Place a line of masking tape on the floor a few feet from the wall at one end of the room.

3. Place six inflated balloons behind the line of tape. Use large balls if a child is afraid of balloons.

4. Place a line of masking tape a few feet from the wall at the other end of the room.

Put a laundry basket or large box behind this line of tape.

5. The first team of two people starts behind the line of masking tape where the balloons are. They place one balloon between them, holding it in place with their hips and legs. They are not allowed to touch the balloon with their hands.

6. The timekeeper begins timing as the team proceeds to move across the room with the balloon between them to drop it in the basket or box. If they touch the balloon or it falls, they need to go back and start again.

7. After dropping the first balloon into the basket, the pair goes back to get another.

8. They continue until all six balloons have been successfully moved to the box.

9. Write down the time it took for the team to move all six balloons.

10. Return the balloons to the starting point.

11. Then the second team has a turn. When the teams of pairs have finished, the timekeeper chooses a partner and takes a turn as well.

12. Add up the scores of each team to get a total score for the whole family.

13. Repeat the game using different pairs. See if your family can better its score.

41 *Me First*

Cooperating

Play game 41 to help children practice coping with not being first all the time.

Set-up

Space to play
Paper and marker
Masking tape
Timer
Lively music (radio or recorded music)

Directions

1. On the paper, write a number for each family member, starting with one.

2. Next, put a family member's name next to each number. All family members must decide together and agree on whose name should go by which number. Who gets to go first? Who goes second? Who goes last?

3. Tape the list to the wall.

4. Make a line-up with person number one at the front. Everyone holds the shoulders, belt, or knees of the person in front.

5. Set the timer for one minute.

6. Turn on the music and follow the leader, as she or he dances through the room.

7. When the timer rings, number one goes to the back of the line; number two is first.

8. Continue until everyone has had a chance to be first.

Solving Problems

Working together to solve a problem is an important skill for families. It requires the use of all the previous skills you have practiced. To solve problems, family members need to be able to cooperate, make and keep agreements, make plans, acknowledge one another's strengths, follow directions, take "no" for an answer, listen to each other's ideas, make requests, respect boundaries, and feel safe with one another. If you have trouble solving problems, see if your family needs more practice in one or two of these other areas.

There is a certain team feeling you get when your family solves a problem together. That feeling of being a team makes family members feel connected and gives them a sense of belonging. Children who feel connected within their own family are more successful in making friends and in making a positive contribution to their community.

Play these games if you want family members to:

♦ Use all of the previously learned skills effectively
♦ Learn how to solve problems without fighting or arguing
♦ Communicate with one another directly instead of tattling
♦ Learn how to work things out instead of being a bully or a victim
♦ Feel connected by having the experience of solving problems together successfully
♦ Trust other family members' abilities to solve problems

- Be able to work things out so everyone feels like a winner

Tips for Solving Problems

- Check and see if there are any prior skills that need more practice. You will notice that solving problems requires many of the previously practiced skills.
- Give children the message that problems can be solved if you work together.
- Your family may need more practice with listening and acknowledging skills, if you find yourself or your children arguing and trying to be right.
- Take the time to solve problems together, and give children the message that their ideas are valued.

Solving problems may at first seem to take up so much time. It would be faster and easier if one person just took over and solved them alone.

Keep in mind that children who have their problems solved for them learn to be either dependent or rebellious. As teenagers, those who are dependent may follow their peers without thinking for themselves. Those who are rebellious . . . well, you can probably imagine what they might do.

43 *Obstacle Course*

Solving Problems

Play game 43 to develop trust in other family members' abilities to solve problems.

Set-up

Space to set up an obstacle course
Blindfold
Pillows, shoes, books, etc.

Directions

1. Set up an obstacle course in the room, using furniture, pillows, shoes, books, and other items.

2. Choose one family member to be the first player.

3. This person is blindfolded and stands at one side of the room.

4. All the other family members help the blindfolded player walk through the obstacles until she touches the wall on the other side of the room. Family members may touch her to guide her.

5. Repeat the game until everyone has had a turn. Change the obstacles around a bit each time.

6. To vary this game, do not touch the blindfolded player, but instead guide her through the obstacles using words only.

44 Divvy Up

Solving Problems

Play game 44 to practice solving the problem of not having enough to go around.

Set-up

Space to play

Basket or bowl for each family member

Bag containing treasures: candies, toys, balls, costume jewelry, pretty stones, etc. Can all be same or different. You will need two items for each family member.

Directions

1. Sit in a circle in chairs or on the floor.

2. Remove one item from the bag of treasures and set it aside.

3. Empty the bag of treasures in the center of the circle of people.

4. Each family member takes one empty bowl or basket.

5. Decide together how to divide the items in the circle among the family members' baskets or bowls. Do not leave any item in the circle.

5. Repeat the game using different items.

Note: With one item "extra," you will have to decide on some way besides just giving everyone two items to solve this problem.

45 *Pillow Challenge*

Solving Problems

Play game 45 to practice working together as a family to solve a problem.

Set-up

Space to play indoors
Two pillows or cushions for each family member

Directions

1. Place all the pillows and people so they are touching the wall at one side of the room.

2. Your intent is to get all the pillows and all the people to the wall at the other side of the room while observing these rules:

- ◆ Only one person can move at a time. All others must remain still. After one person moves, another one may move.

- ◆ A person can only move if she or he is touching another person. Only the moving person needs to be touching someone else. Other players do not have to be touching anyone until they start to move.

- ◆ Each person can touch only one pillow at a time.

- ◆ Pillows not touching a wall must be in contact with a person at all times. Do not throw the pillows.

(Continued on the next page)

◆ Pillows can only touch the floor if they are against the wall. Otherwise, they must be touching a person and not touching the floor.

3. Work together to figure out how to accomplish the goal of getting people and pillows to the other side of the room.

Note: Practice the previous ten skills you have learned in solving this challenge.

46 *Kids Rule*

Solving Problems

Play game 46 to encourage brothers and sisters to solve their problems without seeking their parents' help.

Set-up

Space to play
Space for parents to sit at the side of the room
One magazine for each parent
Stack of newspapers
Two paper bags
Masking tape
Timer

Directions

1. Set these items in the middle of the room: newspapers, two paper bags, masking tape.

2. Parents go to the side of the room to read magazines. They do not pay any attention to the children. This is a chance for the children to practice problem solving without their parents' help.

3. Set the timer for five minutes.

4. Children work together to invent the rules of a game that the whole family could play with the items.

5. When the timer rings the youngest child in the family explains the rules of the game to the parents.

6. Set the timer for five minutes again. Everyone plays the game that the children invented.

7. The children may revise the rules to make the game more successful.

8. Play again if you wish.

Resolving Conflicts

Children often have more energy than their parents do. Sometimes they find that generating a conflict (power struggle) is one way to raise their parents' energy level. Parents need to help children find more appropriate ways to channel their intense energy. Getting physical exercise is an important way to accomplish this. Encourage your children to do things with their whole bodies, such as swimming, biking, climbing, sports, playing outside on the playground equipment (trikes, wagons, swings, monkey bars, etc.). These activities are far preferable to television and videos or interminable computer games.

People get angry when threatened or blocked from achieving their intentions. The tendency is to attack or run away. It is impossible to resolve a conflict when angry. First, we must find a way to calm down. Many techniques are useful: taking several deep breaths, going for a walk, cleaning house, bouncing a ball, doing exercises, and meditating are a few.

Once calm, staying with a problem to work things out is still not an easy task. It requires mastery of all eleven of the previous family skills. When those skills are mastered, families can use them to deal with situations that come up. Conflicts occur less often and can be dealt with better when they do arise.

It is important for all of us to learn to resolve conflicts within the safety and trustworthiness of our own families. Then we can take these skills out to our playgrounds, schools, communities, and relationships with people all over the world.

Play these games if you want family members to:

- Express angry feelings safely
- Learn how to use disagreements to practice using the previous eleven skills
- Practice negotiation
- Dissolve fear of disagreement or conflict
- Have fun and enjoy the fact that people are different
- Be good sports and practice competing in an enjoyable way

Tips for Resolving Conflicts

- Use intense games to play out conflict in a safe way. Games with rules keep people from getting hurt and at the same time allow intense feelings to be expressed, such as in "tug of war."
- Help family members redirect intense feelings and anger into a safe physical outlet.
- Calm down before you try to resolve conflicts when you are angry. When you are calm, use all the skills you have learned to solve the problem.

- Make sure everyone wins, using all the preceding skills. Everyone will feel like a winner when the problem is genuinely resolved.
- Have fun!

47 Tug of War

Resolving Conflicts
Play game 47 to release tensions physically and have fun at the same time.

Set-up
Space to play
Ten-foot rope or jump rope or long, sturdy scarf
Masking tape

Directions:
1. Divide your family into two teams.

2. Place a five-foot line of masking tape on the floor to mark the mid-point between the two teams.

3. Sit on the floor with one team facing the other, about four feet apart, on opposite sides of the tape line.

4. Have each team take hold of one end of the rope or scarf.

5. On a signal decided by the family, each side begins to pull. Pull until one of the teams is pulled over the line of tape into the territory of the other team.

6. Repeat the tug of war, this time choosing different teams.

48 *Pot of Gold*

Resolving Conflicts

Play game 48 to practice negotiating skills among all family members.

Set-up

Space to play
Masking tape
Pillow

Directions:

1. Place a small pillow in the center of the room. Pretend that this pillow has great value and is very desirable.

2. Place two lines of masking tape across the floor one foot from either side of the pillow.

3. Two players stand or sit outside the lines of tape while other family members watch.

4. The players use words only to reach an agreement about how they will each get the pillow. Neither one is allowed to cross the line to pick it up until they have an agreement.

5. Those watching can make suggestions to help the players come to an agreement.

6. Once an agreement is reached and the problem is solved, have a different pair of players repeat the game.

7. Continue until all players have had a turn negotiating for the valuable item.

49 *Paper Ball Battle*

Resolving Conflicts

Play game 49 to provide everyone with a playful, safe outlet for anger and tension.

Set-up

Space to play
Masking tape
Stacks of newspapers
Place to wash newspaper ink off hands

Directions

1. Each player picks a spot and makes a masking tape boundary for him- or herself.

2. Each person places a stack of newspapers within the boundary.

3. Set the timer for one minute. Each player makes as many paper balls as possible. Stop when the timer rings.

4. Set the timer for two minutes now.

5. Everyone throws paper balls at everyone else for two minutes. Players must stay in their boundaries and can throw any balls that land in their boundary or that they can reach from within their boundary.

7. Play goes on until the timer rings or as long as players have balls. Anyone who runs out of balls waits within his boundary.

50 *Hot Air*

Resolving Conflicts
Play game 50 to practice competing in an enjoyable way and being a good sport.

Set-up
Floor or table space to play
Masking tape
Cotton balls

Directions
1. Place two masking tape strips across the middle of a table or on the floor about two feet apart.

2. Divide your family into two teams and give each player five cotton balls.

3. Each team sits or lies down on opposite sides of the masking tape strips.

4. Set the timer for two minutes.

5. Players try to blow their cotton balls to the opposite team's side of the tape. The winning team is the one with the fewest remaining cotton balls when the timer rings.

6. Play again, mixing up the teams.

Note: For variety, you can use other items, such as small balloons, table tennis balls, tissue, small feathers.

Beyond Play

Once you play these skill-building games, you become aware that these skills are the ones you use every day in social situations.

We practice:

- feeling safe and relaxed (trusting) each time we try to fit in when we enter a room full of people we do not know.
- respecting boundaries when we stand in line at the bank or follow the car in front of us at a safe distance.
- making requests when we ask for a raise or for a refund or to exchange something.
- listening when we deal with someone whose ideas and values are different from our own.
- taking "no" for an answer when we forego that second helping of food or realize that we cannot do everything we wanted to.
- acknowledging others when someone helps us out.
- planning when we look over our schedules and try to fit everything in.

- making and keeping agreements when we meet our friend for lunch.
- cooperating when we work on community projects.
- solving problems when we have to transport everyone in our family to several different locations at the same time.
- resolving conflicts when we are angry and frustrated, yet realize the importance of calming down and using our other skills to work things out.

When you play these games, you may still have many questions about why members of your family behave as they do. A parent educator or family coach or counselor can help you understand such issues and find a way to resolve them.

I hope you have had as much fun playing these games as I did inventing them for the families I work with. After playing these games for a while, you will be able to invent games of your own to help your family practice skills they need. Always remember to have fun!

Index

Order these books for quick ideas

Tools for Everyday Parenting Series

Illustrated. Paperback, $11.95 each; library binding, $18.95 each

These books are geared for new or frustrated parents. Fun to look at and fun to read, they present information in both words and cartoons. They are perfect for parents who may be busy with school, jobs, or other responsibilities and who have little time to read.

Magic Tools for Raising Kids, by Elizabeth Crary * Parenting young children is easier and more effective with a toolbox of useful, child-tested, positive tools. Learn what to do, how to do it, and what to say to make raising lovable, self-confident kids easier. 128 pages, ISBN 0-943990-77-7 paperback, 0-943990-78-5 library

365 Wacky, Wonderful Ways to Get Your Children to Do What You Want, by Elizabeth Crary * Young children share certain behaviors that are calculated to drive parents crazy. Here are hundreds of practical (and sometimes zany) ideas to help parents cope. 104 pages, ISBN 0-943990-79-3 paperback, 0-943990-80-7 library

Ask for these books at your favorite bookstore, or call toll free 1-800-992-6657. VISA and MasterCard accepted with phone orders. Complete book catalog available on request.

Parenting Press, Inc., Dept. 202, P.O. Box 75267, Seattle, WA 98175
www.ParentingPress.com

In Canada, call **Raincoast Books Distributing Co.**, 1-800-663-5714.
Prices subject to change without notice